Bananas Farm to Home

Table of Contents

by Liz Ray

Getting Started

Do you ever wonder where your food comes from? Perhaps the peppers you ate for dinner were grown in Mexico. The cocoa you drank may have come from Africa.

Some of the food you eat is grown in our own country. Some of it comes from far away. To learn more about how foods "travel," let's take a look at the bananas in your kitchen.

Most bananas grow in other parts of the world. Perhaps your bananas came from South America. So how did they end up in your kitchen? Let's find out!

Growing and Harvesting

Bananas grow where the weather is warm and rainy. It takes the right kind of weather and a lot of hard work to grow good bananas.

To grow bananas, **workers** must first clear the land. Then they can plant the banana seeds. If there is not enough rain, the workers have to water the banana plants.

Bananas become heavy as they grow. A banana plant must be propped up so the fruit doesn't pull it down. Workers cover each banana bunch with a plastic bag. The bags protect the bananas from bugs, birds, and wind.

Bananas are **harvested**, or picked, when they are green and hard. One worker cuts the bananas from the plant. Another worker attaches the bananas to a cable or puts them in a cart. Then the bananas are taken to a packing shed.

In the packing shed, the bananas are washed and sorted. Then workers pack the fruit in cardboard boxes. Now the bananas are ready to **transport**.

Transporting and Exporting

Many of the bananas grown in South America are **exported**. That means they are sent to other countries.

Transporting bananas for export is tricky. Bananas must be kept cool so they do not ripen too quickly. Bananas must be handled gently to prevent bruises.

Special trucks take the bananas from the farm. The trucks are refrigerated. They keep the bananas cool on the way to the port for shipping.

At the port, workers carefully unload the boxes of bananas from the trucks. Then they load the boxes onto ships. The ships are also refrigerated.

Time to Ripen

The ships bring the fruit to ports in this country. There workers unload the boxes of bananas. Then the bananas are taken to banana ripening rooms.

These special rooms are the perfect place to ripen the green bananas. The ripening rooms are not too cold or too hot. They are not too dry or too damp. A special gas is used to help ripen the fruit in just the right way.

Now the bananas are ready for market. They are again loaded onto trucks. Truck drivers take the fruit to stores and supermarkets.

At the store, the fruit is unloaded from the truck. Clerks put the bananas on shelves. The bananas are now ready for **consumers**. Who is a consumer? You are!

From Farm to Home

Consumers are people who use food or anything else that is grown or made by others. We consume many things such as food, clothes, and cars.

Many of the things we use are made in this country. Many others are made in other parts of the world. It takes a lot of people working together to bring us the things we use.

The next time you buy bananas at the store, stop and think. From farmers to truck drivers to store clerks—many people worked hard to bring those bananas to you!

How Bananas Get From the Farm to You

Bananas are:

1. planted and grown

2. harvested

3. washed, sorted, and packed

4. transported to ships

5. shipped to new ports

6. ripened

7. transported to stores

8. sold to consumers

Index